WEDDING TASKS

THIS BOOK BELONGS TO

_____

Wedding Tasks

WEDDING:

SCHEDULE OF EVENTS

FOR THE BRIDE

FOR THE GROOM

Wedding Tasks

WEDDING:

SCHEDULE OF EVENTS

FOR THE BRIDE

FOR THE GROOM

Wedding Tasks

WEDDING:

SCHEDULE OF EVENTS

FOR THE BRIDE

FOR THE GROOM

Wedding Tasks

WEDDING:

SCHEDULE OF EVENTS

FOR THE BRIDE

FOR THE GROOM

Wedding Tasks

WEDDING:

SCHEDULE OF EVENTS

FOR THE BRIDE

FOR THE GROOM

Wedding Tasks

WEDDING:

SCHEDULE OF EVENTS

FOR THE BRIDE

FOR THE GROOM

Wedding Tasks

WEDDING:

SCHEDULE OF EVENTS

FOR THE BRIDE

FOR THE GROOM

Wedding Tasks

WEDDING:

SCHEDULE OF EVENTS

FOR THE BRIDE

FOR THE GROOM

Wedding Tasks

WEDDING:

SCHEDULE OF EVENTS

FOR THE BRIDE

FOR THE GROOM

Wedding Tasks

WEDDING:

SCHEDULE OF EVENTS

FOR THE BRIDE

FOR THE GROOM

Wedding Tasks

WEDDING:

SCHEDULE OF EVENTS

FOR THE BRIDE

FOR THE GROOM

Wedding Tasks

WEDDING:

SCHEDULE OF EVENTS

FOR THE BRIDE

FOR THE GROOM

Wedding Tasks

WEDDING:

SCHEDULE OF EVENTS

FOR THE BRIDE

FOR THE GROOM

Wedding Tasks

WEDDING:

SCHEDULE OF EVENTS

FOR THE BRIDE

FOR THE GROOM

Wedding Tasks

WEDDING:

SCHEDULE OF EVENTS

FOR THE BRIDE

FOR THE GROOM

Wedding Tasks

WEDDING:

SCHEDULE OF EVENTS

FOR THE BRIDE

FOR THE GROOM

Wedding Tasks

WEDDING:

SCHEDULE OF EVENTS

FOR THE BRIDE

FOR THE GROOM

Wedding Tasks

WEDDING:

SCHEDULE OF EVENTS

FOR THE BRIDE

FOR THE GROOM

Wedding Tasks

WEDDING:

SCHEDULE OF EVENTS

FOR THE BRIDE

FOR THE GROOM

Wedding Tasks

WEDDING:

SCHEDULE OF EVENTS

FOR THE BRIDE

FOR THE GROOM

Wedding Tasks

WEDDING:

SCHEDULE OF EVENTS

FOR THE BRIDE

FOR THE GROOM

Wedding Tasks

WEDDING:

SCHEDULE OF EVENTS

FOR THE BRIDE

FOR THE GROOM

Wedding Tasks

WEDDING:

SCHEDULE OF EVENTS

FOR THE BRIDE

FOR THE GROOM

Wedding Tasks

WEDDING:

SCHEDULE OF EVENTS

FOR THE BRIDE

FOR THE GROOM

Wedding Tasks

WEDDING:

SCHEDULE OF EVENTS

FOR THE BRIDE

FOR THE GROOM

Wedding Tasks

WEDDING:

SCHEDULE OF EVENTS

FOR THE BRIDE

FOR THE GROOM

Wedding Tasks

WEDDING:

SCHEDULE OF EVENTS

FOR THE BRIDE

FOR THE GROOM

Wedding Tasks

WEDDING:

SCHEDULE OF EVENTS

FOR THE BRIDE

FOR THE GROOM

Wedding Tasks

WEDDING:

SCHEDULE OF EVENTS

FOR THE BRIDE

FOR THE GROOM

Wedding Tasks

WEDDING:

SCHEDULE OF EVENTS

FOR THE BRIDE

FOR THE GROOM

Wedding Tasks

WEDDING:

SCHEDULE OF EVENTS

FOR THE BRIDE

FOR THE GROOM

Wedding Tasks

WEDDING:

SCHEDULE OF EVENTS

FOR THE BRIDE

FOR THE GROOM

Wedding Tasks

WEDDING:

SCHEDULE OF EVENTS

FOR THE BRIDE

FOR THE GROOM

Wedding Tasks

WEDDING:

SCHEDULE OF EVENTS

FOR THE BRIDE

FOR THE GROOM

Wedding Tasks

WEDDING:

SCHEDULE OF EVENTS

FOR THE BRIDE

FOR THE GROOM

Wedding Tasks

WEDDING:

SCHEDULE OF EVENTS

FOR THE BRIDE

FOR THE GROOM

Wedding Tasks

WEDDING:

SCHEDULE OF EVENTS

FOR THE BRIDE

FOR THE GROOM

Wedding Tasks

WEDDING:

SCHEDULE OF EVENTS

FOR THE BRIDE

FOR THE GROOM

Wedding Tasks

WEDDING:

SCHEDULE OF EVENTS

FOR THE BRIDE

FOR THE GROOM

Wedding Tasks

WEDDING:

SCHEDULE OF EVENTS

FOR THE BRIDE

FOR THE GROOM

Wedding Tasks

WEDDING:

SCHEDULE OF EVENTS

FOR THE BRIDE

FOR THE GROOM

Wedding Tasks

WEDDING:

SCHEDULE OF EVENTS

FOR THE BRIDE

FOR THE GROOM

Wedding Tasks

WEDDING:

SCHEDULE OF EVENTS

FOR THE BRIDE

FOR THE GROOM

Wedding Tasks

WEDDING:

SCHEDULE OF EVENTS

FOR THE BRIDE

FOR THE GROOM

Wedding Tasks

WEDDING:

SCHEDULE OF EVENTS

FOR THE BRIDE

FOR THE GROOM

Wedding Tasks

WEDDING:

SCHEDULE OF EVENTS

FOR THE BRIDE

FOR THE GROOM

Wedding Tasks

WEDDING:

SCHEDULE OF EVENTS

FOR THE BRIDE

FOR THE GROOM

Wedding Tasks

WEDDING:

SCHEDULE OF EVENTS

FOR THE BRIDE

FOR THE GROOM

Wedding Tasks

WEDDING:

SCHEDULE OF EVENTS

FOR THE BRIDE

FOR THE GROOM

Wedding Tasks

WEDDING:

SCHEDULE OF EVENTS

FOR THE BRIDE

FOR THE GROOM

Wedding Tasks

WEDDING:

SCHEDULE OF EVENTS

FOR THE BRIDE

FOR THE GROOM

Wedding Tasks

WEDDING:

SCHEDULE OF EVENTS

FOR THE BRIDE

FOR THE GROOM

Wedding Tasks

WEDDING:

SCHEDULE OF EVENTS

FOR THE BRIDE

FOR THE GROOM

Wedding Tasks

WEDDING:

SCHEDULE OF EVENTS

FOR THE BRIDE

FOR THE GROOM

Wedding Tasks

WEDDING:

SCHEDULE OF EVENTS

FOR THE BRIDE

FOR THE GROOM

Wedding Tasks

WEDDING:

SCHEDULE OF EVENTS

FOR THE BRIDE

FOR THE GROOM

Wedding Tasks

WEDDING:

SCHEDULE OF EVENTS

FOR THE BRIDE

FOR THE GROOM

Wedding Tasks

WEDDING:

SCHEDULE OF EVENTS

FOR THE BRIDE

FOR THE GROOM

Wedding Tasks

WEDDING:

SCHEDULE OF EVENTS

FOR THE BRIDE

FOR THE GROOM

Wedding Tasks

WEDDING:

SCHEDULE OF EVENTS

FOR THE BRIDE

FOR THE GROOM

Wedding Tasks

WEDDING:

SCHEDULE OF EVENTS

FOR THE BRIDE

FOR THE GROOM

Wedding Tasks

WEDDING:

SCHEDULE OF EVENTS

FOR THE BRIDE

FOR THE GROOM

Wedding Tasks

WEDDING:

SCHEDULE OF EVENTS

FOR THE BRIDE

FOR THE GROOM

Wedding Tasks

WEDDING:

SCHEDULE OF EVENTS

FOR THE BRIDE

FOR THE GROOM

Wedding Tasks

WEDDING:

SCHEDULE OF EVENTS

FOR THE BRIDE

FOR THE GROOM

Wedding Tasks

WEDDING:

SCHEDULE OF EVENTS

FOR THE BRIDE

FOR THE GROOM

Wedding Tasks

WEDDING:

SCHEDULE OF EVENTS

FOR THE BRIDE

FOR THE GROOM

Wedding Tasks

WEDDING:

SCHEDULE OF EVENTS

FOR THE BRIDE

FOR THE GROOM

Wedding Tasks

WEDDING:

SCHEDULE OF EVENTS

FOR THE BRIDE

FOR THE GROOM

Wedding Tasks

WEDDING:

SCHEDULE OF EVENTS

FOR THE BRIDE

FOR THE GROOM

Wedding Tasks

WEDDING:

SCHEDULE OF EVENTS

FOR THE BRIDE

FOR THE GROOM

Wedding Tasks

WEDDING:

SCHEDULE OF EVENTS

FOR THE BRIDE

FOR THE GROOM

Wedding Tasks

WEDDING:

SCHEDULE OF EVENTS

FOR THE BRIDE

FOR THE GROOM

Wedding Tasks

WEDDING:

SCHEDULE OF EVENTS

FOR THE BRIDE

FOR THE GROOM

Wedding Tasks

WEDDING:

SCHEDULE OF EVENTS

FOR THE BRIDE

FOR THE GROOM

Wedding Tasks

WEDDING:

SCHEDULE OF EVENTS

FOR THE BRIDE

FOR THE GROOM

Wedding Tasks

WEDDING:

SCHEDULE OF EVENTS

FOR THE BRIDE

FOR THE GROOM

Wedding Tasks

WEDDING:

SCHEDULE OF EVENTS

FOR THE BRIDE

FOR THE GROOM

Wedding Tasks

WEDDING:

SCHEDULE OF EVENTS

FOR THE BRIDE

FOR THE GROOM

Wedding Tasks

WEDDING:

SCHEDULE OF EVENTS

FOR THE BRIDE

FOR THE GROOM

Wedding Tasks

WEDDING:

SCHEDULE OF EVENTS

FOR THE BRIDE

FOR THE GROOM

Wedding Tasks

WEDDING:

SCHEDULE OF EVENTS

FOR THE BRIDE

FOR THE GROOM

Wedding Tasks

WEDDING:

SCHEDULE OF EVENTS

FOR THE BRIDE

FOR THE GROOM

Wedding Tasks

WEDDING:

SCHEDULE OF EVENTS

FOR THE BRIDE

FOR THE GROOM

Wedding Tasks

WEDDING:

SCHEDULE OF EVENTS

FOR THE BRIDE

FOR THE GROOM

Wedding Tasks

WEDDING:

SCHEDULE OF EVENTS

FOR THE BRIDE

FOR THE GROOM

Wedding Tasks

WEDDING:

SCHEDULE OF EVENTS

FOR THE BRIDE

FOR THE GROOM

Wedding Tasks

WEDDING:

SCHEDULE OF EVENTS

FOR THE BRIDE

FOR THE GROOM

Wedding Tasks

WEDDING:

SCHEDULE OF EVENTS

FOR THE BRIDE

FOR THE GROOM

Wedding Tasks

WEDDING:

SCHEDULE OF EVENTS

FOR THE BRIDE

FOR THE GROOM

Wedding Tasks

WEDDING:

SCHEDULE OF EVENTS

FOR THE BRIDE

FOR THE GROOM

Wedding Tasks

WEDDING:

SCHEDULE OF EVENTS

FOR THE BRIDE

FOR THE GROOM

Wedding Tasks

WEDDING:

SCHEDULE OF EVENTS

FOR THE BRIDE

FOR THE GROOM

Wedding Tasks

WEDDING:

SCHEDULE OF EVENTS

FOR THE BRIDE

FOR THE GROOM

Wedding Tasks

WEDDING:

SCHEDULE OF EVENTS

FOR THE BRIDE

FOR THE GROOM

Wedding Tasks

WEDDING:

SCHEDULE OF EVENTS

FOR THE BRIDE

FOR THE GROOM

Wedding Tasks

WEDDING:

SCHEDULE OF EVENTS

FOR THE BRIDE

FOR THE GROOM

Wedding Tasks

WEDDING:

SCHEDULE OF EVENTS

FOR THE BRIDE

FOR THE GROOM

Wedding Tasks

WEDDING:

SCHEDULE OF EVENTS

FOR THE BRIDE

FOR THE GROOM

Wedding Tasks

WEDDING:

SCHEDULE OF EVENTS

FOR THE BRIDE

FOR THE GROOM

Wedding Tasks

WEDDING:

SCHEDULE OF EVENTS

FOR THE BRIDE

FOR THE GROOM

Wedding Tasks

WEDDING:

SCHEDULE OF EVENTS

FOR THE BRIDE

FOR THE GROOM

Wedding Tasks

WEDDING:

SCHEDULE OF EVENTS

FOR THE BRIDE

FOR THE GROOM

Wedding Tasks

WEDDING:

SCHEDULE OF EVENTS

FOR THE BRIDE

FOR THE GROOM

Wedding Tasks

WEDDING:

SCHEDULE OF EVENTS

FOR THE BRIDE

FOR THE GROOM

Wedding Tasks

WEDDING:

SCHEDULE OF EVENTS

FOR THE BRIDE

FOR THE GROOM

Wedding Tasks

WEDDING:

SCHEDULE OF EVENTS

FOR THE BRIDE

FOR THE GROOM

Wedding Tasks

WEDDING:

SCHEDULE OF EVENTS

FOR THE BRIDE

FOR THE GROOM

Wedding Tasks

WEDDING:

SCHEDULE OF EVENTS

FOR THE BRIDE

FOR THE GROOM

Wedding Tasks

WEDDING:

SCHEDULE OF EVENTS

FOR THE BRIDE

FOR THE GROOM

Wedding Tasks

WEDDING:

SCHEDULE OF EVENTS

FOR THE BRIDE

FOR THE GROOM

Wedding Tasks

WEDDING:

SCHEDULE OF EVENTS

FOR THE BRIDE

FOR THE GROOM

Wedding Tasks

WEDDING:

SCHEDULE OF EVENTS

FOR THE BRIDE

FOR THE GROOM

Wedding Tasks

WEDDING:

SCHEDULE OF EVENTS

FOR THE BRIDE

FOR THE GROOM

Wedding Tasks

WEDDING:

SCHEDULE OF EVENTS

FOR THE BRIDE

FOR THE GROOM

Wedding Tasks

WEDDING:

SCHEDULE OF EVENTS

FOR THE BRIDE

FOR THE GROOM

Wedding Tasks

WEDDING:

SCHEDULE OF EVENTS

FOR THE BRIDE

FOR THE GROOM

Wedding Tasks

WEDDING:

SCHEDULE OF EVENTS

FOR THE BRIDE

FOR THE GROOM

Wedding Tasks

WEDDING:

SCHEDULE OF EVENTS

FOR THE BRIDE

FOR THE GROOM

www.ingramcontent.com/pod-product-compliance
Lightning Source LLC
LaVergne TN
LVHW080048220125
801834LV00036B/1022